LAND OF THE FREE

The U.S. Capitol

Anne Hempstead

Heinemann Library
Chicago, Illinois

© 2006 Heinemann
Published by Heinemann Library
A division of Reed Elsevier Inc.
Chicago, IL
Customer Service 888-363-4266
Visit our website at www.heinemannraintree.com

For more information address the publisher:
Raintree, 100 N. LaSalle, Suite 1200, Chicago IL 60602

Printed in China by WKT Company Limited

10 09 08 07 06
10 9 8 7 6 5 4 3 2 1

ISBN 1-4034-7000-6 (hc) -- ISBN 1-4034-7007-3 (pb)

Library of Congress Cataloging-in-Publication Data:

Cataloging-in-publication data is on file at the Library of Congress.

Photo research: Julie Laffin

Acknowledgments
The author and publisher are grateful to the following for permission to reproduce copyright material:
pp. 4, 7, 20 Corbis, p.8, 17 The Granger Collection, p. 10, 24 Corbis/Bettmann, p.12, 15, Library of Congress, p.14 Maryland Historical Society, p.18 Corbis/Charles O'Rear, p.23 Corbis/Wally Mcnamee, p.27 Andrew E. Cook.

Cover Photo: ©Heinemann-Raintree/Jill Birschbach

Every effort has been made to contact the copyright holders of any material reproduced in this book. Any omissions will be rectified in subsequent printings if notice is given to the publishers.

The paper used to print this book comes from sustainable resources.

Contents

What is Congress?

Congress consists of the Senate and the House of Representatives (often called the House). Each state has two senators. The number of State Representatives depends on the population of the state. Seven states have only one representative each, whereas a large state like California has 53. Citizens in each state elect their members of Congress.

Chapter One:
Symbol of Democracy

The U.S. Capitol building is the workplace of Congress, which is the **legislative**, or law-making, branch of the U.S. government. Members of Congress meet in the Capitol's Senate and House **chambers**, committee rooms, and offices to **debate** and vote for the laws of the United States.

In addition to serving as a meeting place for Congress, the Capitol has other important uses. It is a museum with a fine collection of American paintings and statues of famous people. It is used as a **patriotic** and dignified setting for special government ceremonies. The Capitol is also a popular tourist attraction. Millions of visitors have come to admire its beautiful dome and walk its historic halls.

The Capitol is more than a building. For the nation and many people around the world, the Capitol is a respected and hopeful symbol of freedom and justice. It is the home of American **democracy**.

Washington, D.C.: Home to the Capitol

The Capitol building is located in Washington, D.C., the capital city of the United States. Washington serves as the center of the national government. Along with hundreds of government offices, Washington has important museums, monuments, and landmarks dedicated to American history, art, and culture. Just like any large city, Washington also has homes, schools, stores, and private businesses. However, Washington's biggest business is the U. S. Government.

Measuring 751 feet 4 inches (229 meters 10 centimeters) long and 350 feet (107 meters) wide at its greatest width, the Capitol building is a huge structure. It is a little more than two football fields long and a little more than one football field wide. The great white dome rises 288 feet (69 meters) up into the sky. Starting at the basement level, you have to climb 365 steps to reach the very top. Its 5 floor levels provide over 16 1/2 acres of space divided into a maze of halls and 540 rooms. There are 658 windows to wash. The marble columns, elegant **chambers**, and cast iron dome topped with the Statue of Freedom all make the Capitol an amazing work of **architecture**.

A capital capitol

The words *capital* and *capitol* sound the same, but mean different things. *Capital*, spelled with an *a*, refers to the head of something. A capital city is where the government of a state or country meets. *Capitol*, spelled with an *o*, refers to a building where a law-making group meets. When *capitol* is spelled with an uppercase *C*, it specifically refers to the U.S. Capitol building.

This view of Washington from the air shows the layout of Capitol Hill.

The Capitol is so big it has been called "a little city within itself." The building has its own post office, stores, printing offices, and police. Members of Congress can consult a doctor in the medical facility, argue politics over a hamburger in one of its restaurants, or step into the prayer room for a quiet moment. More than 20,000 men and women assist the 535 members of Congress as they carry out their law-making duties. All together, the total number of people working in the Capitol could populate a small town. Every year, 3 to 5 million visitors come to the nation's Capitol to see **democracy** at work.

1791

Chapter Two: A Capital City for a New Nation

After the Revolutionary War, many challenges lay ahead for the United States. When Congress met in New York in 1789, one of the biggest questions was where to locate the capital city. Since 1774, when the First Continental Congress was held in Philadelphia, Pennsylvania, the government had moved thirteen times and met in eight different cities. If the new nation was to be stable and lasting, the government needed a permanent home.

Everyone knew how important this city would become to the nation and the world, but they had different opinions about where it should be. New Englanders wanted New York City to be the capital. Southerners pushed for locating it in the South, while people from Pennsylvania argued for Philadelphia. The **debate** became so fierce that when the decision to have the capital in Philadelphia was up for a vote, two Southern congressmen went to the home of Samuel Johnston, a senator from North Carolina who was ill at the time. They carried him in a chair to the Senate **chamber**, so that Johnston, still wearing his nightcap, could cast his defeating vote against Philadelphia.

Finally a compromise was reached. In 1790 Congress voted for a capital city to be established along the Potomac River between Maryland and Virginia. Locating the city at the midpoint of the country seemed to be fair. The new capital would not be part of any state. It would have its own 10-square-mile (26-square-kilometer) area designated Washington, District of Columbia. Congress put President George Washington in charge of choosing the exact site for the city. Congress ordered that both a meetinghouse for Congress and a home for the president be built and completed by 1800.

This lithograph shows a 19th century view of George Washington's home at Mt. Vernon.

Planning begins

The great capital city building project began. George Washington appointed three men as building and planning supervisors. The group named the new city Washington. The exact boundaries, or limits, of the city had to be established. The supervisors hired Andrew Ellicott, a veteran of the Revolutionary War, and Benjamin Banneker, a mathematician and inventor, to set the boundaries. Banneker helped Ellicott make precise calculations to determine the placement of 40 boundary stones that marked each mile bordering the area.

Washington and other leaders wanted the capital city to serve the practical needs of the government. But they also wanted it to be a **symbol** of the hope and potential of the new nation. George Washington hired a French artist and engineer, Pierre L'Enfant, to plan the city.

World-class city or swamp?

George Washington wanted to locate the capital city on the Potomac, near his plantation Mount Vernon. This decision was not popular with everyone. New Yorkers complained the city would be a "wilderness, peopled with wolves." The site seemed to be in the middle of nowhere. Once inhabited by several Native American tribes, by the 1780s, the area was dotted with a few large houses. Travel to the site was difficult and could be dangerous. When driving from Baltimore, even experienced coachmen were known to get lost in the thick forests on the way.

A vision

L'Enfant imagined a city with magnificent buildings and broad, tree-lined avenues. The new city would be equal to the great capitals in Europe. The city would be a center of **democracy**, where citizens would be able to meet and talk with members of Congress and the president. L'Enfant placed the future home of Congress on Jenkin's Hill in the center of the city to show that the law-making body was the heart of the U.S. government. He extended a 400-foot (122-meter) wide "Grand Avenue" west from the Capitol building to the Potomac River. At the foot of Jenkins Hill, he planned for a public garden with a statue of George

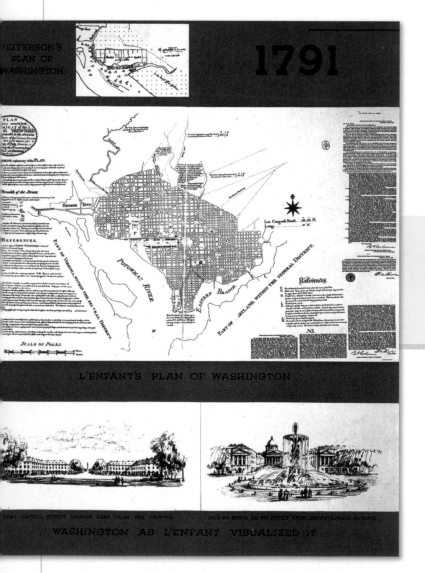

This 20th Century brochure shows L'Enfant's plan for Washington, D.C.

Washington on a horse. To show the separate but equal powers of the two branches of government, L'Enfant placed the president's house directly north of the statue, but linked it to Congress with a mile-long diagonal avenue. The plan was new and original, just like the United States.

L'Enfant had trouble getting along with other people, however, and President Washington ended up firing him from the project before he finished his drawings for the city and its buildings. Andrew Ellicott filled in further details and then hired two artists to add artistic flourishes to the drawings.

Democracy and architecture

Thomas Jefferson, one of the country's founders, and an **amateur architect** and inventor, led the push to rid the country of British influence. He wanted to develop an American style. Jefferson believed that architecture based on Greek and Roman styles would inspire pride. Buildings became a way to display through bricks and mortar the democratic ideals of the ancient societies of Greece and Rome. Domes, temple fronts, columns, and other Greek and Roman details began to be used in the design of homes, churches, and public buildings all over the country. The new American style was called neo-classical or Greek revival.

Designed for democracy

In his design for the city, L'Enfant placed the Congress House on top of a plot of land called Jenkins Hill. However, he never drew the plans for the building itself. Thomas Jefferson suggested that a design contest be held.

In 1792 a competition for the design of the Capitol building was announced. At that time there were very few trained **architects** in the country. Only one professional architect submitted a design. A number of **amateurs**—including two British Revolutionary War veterans, a furniture maker, and a judge—sent in designs. But all the entries were disappointing. Some were poorly drawn while others had odd details.

After the deadline for the contest had passed, a young doctor asked permission to submit his drawings late. Months later, William Thornton presented a plan for a classically styled building. His design looked like a new kind of Roman temple—an American temple of liberty.

This proposal for the design of the Capitol was submitted by James Diamond.

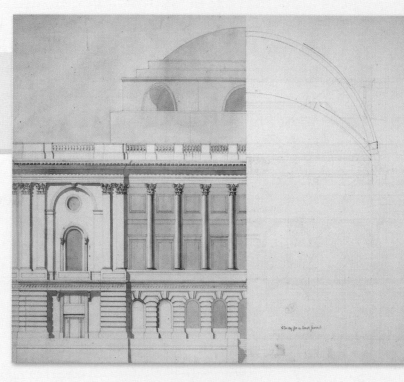

This is one of the submissions for the design of the Capitol.

Thornton placed the meeting chambers for the two houses of Congress in opposing wings. This symbolized the balance of power between the Senate and the House of Representatives. A domed circular room, or **rotunda**, connected the two wings. The rotunda was intended to be a grand public meeting place, a "Hall of the People."

This was exactly how Jefferson and Washington thought the Capitol should be. They praised Thornton's design for its "grandeur, simplicity, and convenience." The plan was immediately approved. On September 18, 1793, George Washington laid the cornerstone for the new Capitol. After an impressive parade and ceremony, the crowd joined Washington on Jenkins Hill for a feast in celebration.

The Capitol was off to a good start, but not for long. Due to lack of money, skilled workers, and materials, construction was very slow moving. In late 1800, Congress, the Supreme Court, and the Library of Congress moved into the North Wing of the far-from-completed building.

Democracy in action

In 1803 Benjamin Henry Latrobe was appointed to complete Thornton's plan. The **architect** devoted his talents to the interior of the building. He finished the grand meeting **chambers** with marble, elegant woodcarvings, and high ceilings. Latrobe added to the building's American style by combining classical marble columns decorated with corn and tobacco designs. This celebrated the native plants and the importance of farming in American life.

In the spirit of **democracy**, Latrobe also added visitors' **galleries** where the public could watch Congress at work. Even before it was finished in 1811, artistic pictures showing a completed building were popular with Americans. The Capitol quickly became a source of national pride.

In 1812 Congress declared war against Great Britain and, in August of 1814, the English marched on Washington, D.C. The British commander was under orders to "destroy and lay waste" to Washington. He was prepared to let the city stand if the Americans paid a ransom. But there was no one to negotiate with. President James Madison and practically everyone else had left town. The soldiers set fire to the city's public buildings.

The War of 1812 (1812-1815)

On June 18, 1812, the United States declared war on Great Britain. The war was a result of several long-term quarrels between the two countries. The war ended in a stalemate, meaning neither side really won. However, the United States's ability to defend itself against Great Britain helped to establish U.S. independence once and for all.

This painting by an unknown artist shows people fleeing the burning city of Washington.

At first the Capitol's stone walls would not catch fire. So the soldiers gathered furniture, books, and tar barrels into piles and put a torch to them. The Capitol went up in flames. The whole city was about to be burned to the ground when a rainstorm put out the fire. The Capitol was left a blackened, gutted shell. The worst damage was in the Senate wing of the building, which had held the books and manuscripts of the Library of Congress.

Newspapers angrily reported the burning of Washington. Americans were outraged, and the Capitol was rebuilt.

In the coming decades, the Capitol fulfilled its promise to become the home of democracy in action. Within its walls, laws and other important decisions concerning taxation, state's rights, and slavery were introduced and often fiercely **debated**. The public crowded the Senate and House galleries to hear great speakers such as Henry Clay, John C. Calhoun, and Daniel Webster present their ideas and opinions on the important issues of the day.

The Capitol and the union of states

By the 1850s, Congress had 62 Senators and 232 Representatives and had outgrown its home again. Thomas Ustick Walter, an **architect** from Philadelphia, won a competition to redesign the Capitol. Walter's plans tripled the building's size by extending both sides with additions that provided new larger **chambers** for both houses. Walter also designed a spectacular dome made of cast iron. The massive dome would weigh nearly 9 million pounds (4 million kilograms).

A statue of freedom

The new dome of the Capitol was to be crowned with a bronze statue of a female figure representing Freedom. The statue became associated with the country's bitter **debate** over slavery. Originally the sculptor depicted Freedom with a liberty cap. The cap was modeled after ones worn by freed slaves in ancient Rome. Jefferson Davis, who was a Senator from Mississippi and would later be the President of the Confederacy,

This photograph of the statue on the Capitol's dome was taken when the statue was removed for cleaning.

protested. Some people thought he felt the cap was an insult to the South. Davis claimed he rejected the cap because Americans were not descended from Roman slaves. The sculptor changed the hat to a headdress of an eagle's head and feathers.

When the Civil War (1861–1865) broke out, construction on the Capitol's dome slowed down, but did not stop. A small group of workers continued working on the building. For a time the Capitol was used as a **barracks** and then a hospital for Union soldiers. Some rooms in the basement became storehouses, while others were used as bakeries.

The Capitol was a symbol of unity and strength of the country. Continuing the work on the building, even though the war was raging, sent an important message to both sides—the Capitol and the union of states would continue. On December 2, 1863, the giant statue of Freedom was raised to the top of the dome and bolted in place. A large U.S. flag fluttered overhead while artillery fired a 35-gun salute, one for every state, including those that had **seceded** from the Union.

The architectural additions of the 1860s, 1880s, and 1890s created the Capitol building we see today. Over the years since then, the building has been remodeled and modernized, but its exterior and great dome have remained unchanged. The designers of the Capitol worked hard to create an inspiring symbol of **democracy**, freedom, and fair government.

Chapter Three: Living History, Working Democracy

Today the Capitol is the thriving center of our working **democracy**. Stepping into the **rotunda**, the great round room under the dome, one is quickly reminded of Thornton's plan for a grand public hall. The huge circular room is nearly 100 feet (30 meters) across and over 180 feet (54 meters) high. The rotunda serves as a busy crossing point in the middle of the building. Representatives, aides, media people, maintenance workers, congressional staffers, visitors, and tourists walk though the rotunda on their way to the Senate and House wings of the building.

The rotunda is also the center of the Capitol's collection of American art. Paintings depicting the early days of discovery and the American Revolution hang on the surrounding walls. On the ceiling is a painting of George Washington rising to heaven. Around the room are statues of the nation's leaders including George Washington, Alexander Hamilton, and Abraham Lincoln.

From the rotunda, a maze of rooms and halls reach into the Senate and House wings. In contrast with the marble exterior, the inside of the Capitol is decorated with colorful paintings. Walking through the many rooms and halls is a journey through American history told through art and **architecture**. The old Senate **Chamber** and the old Supreme Court room are restored to look exactly as they did before 1860.

Congress today

Today, just as in the 1800s, Congress meets in the U.S. Capitol building to make the laws of the country. Almost all members of Congress are also members of one of the two major political parties of the United States, the Republicans and the Democrats. Each party has it own political viewpoint or opinion on issues. Members of Congress usually vote according to their party's viewpoint, but they can also choose to vote with the other party.

Senators meet in the Senate **chamber** where the members sit at desks. There are 100 desks to allow seating for two senators from each state. In addition to voting on legislation, the Senate meets to approve presidential nominations for important government offices such as Secretary of State. The Senate also approves treaties, or agreements, that the president makes with other countries.

The House of Representatives chamber is one of the largest meeting rooms in the world. The population of each state determines its number of representatives. When the House of Representatives grew to 435 people, there was no longer room for a desk for every member. Representatives sit in chairs. Republicans sit to the left of the Speaker of the House and Democrats sit to his right.

Most of the work of Congress is not done in the chambers. It is done by committees in rooms in the Capitol building or one of the newer Congressional office buildings. Both

the Senate and the House have committees such as the
agricultural committee and the armed services committee.
Any member with an idea for a law must introduce it
in Congress as a bill. The bill goes to a committee to be
discussed and voted on. Then it goes to the House and, if
passed there, it goes on to the Senate. Members can vote
with their party or vote across party lines. This is all part of
the democratic process. If passed by both houses, the bill
goes to the president. When the president signs the bill, it
becomes a federal law.

President Bill Clinton giving the 1997
State of the Union address in the House
Chamber.

Chapter Four: The Capitol and the American People

The country's founders wanted a government that was open to the people. Concerned citizens, unions, women's and civil right's organizations, environmentalists, and war protestors have all chosen the Capitol as a place to demonstrate their right to free speech.

Another important part of having access to the government's workings is a free press. Since 1789, the public and the press have been able to attend House **debates** and voting. The Senate admitted the press in 1795. At first, only newspaper reporters were allowed in the Congressional press **galleries**. However, as time passed, advances in technology led to more types of media wanting to cover government proceedings. Now the House and the Senate each have a "daily press gallery" for daily newspapers, a "periodical press gallery" for magazines and other non-daily publications, and a "radio-television gallery" for radio and television reporters. Visitors to the Capitol can get a pass to sit in the public galleries and observe sessions.

Solemn ceremonies

The Capitol is the site for many historic events. Many newly elected presidents take the oath of office on the Capitol steps, as thousands of people gather to watch. Television and radio stations broadcast it to a huge audience beyond Washington. This ceremony shows that the changing of the nation's leaders is done in an orderly and public way.

Because of its beauty and grand size, the **rotunda** is the site of the nation's most solemn occasions. The bodies of late presidents, members of Congress, generals, and national heroes have lain in state in the rotunda after their deaths. This allows admirers to pay their last respects before the funeral. Abraham Lincoln was the first president to be honored in that way. In October 2005 Rosa Parks, a leader of the Civil Rights Movement, was the first woman honored in this way

The Capitol in popular culture

The designers of the Capitol worked hard to create an inspiring symbol of **democracy** and freedom. The building is recognized around the world. It has become an important symbol in popular culture, or the everyday interests and concerns of many people.

Movies that take place in Washington, D.C., almost always feature a screen shot of the Capitol, because it will emphasize where the story is taking place. When people visit Washington, D.C., they can buy souvenirs that feature the building. Not just postcards, but capitol-themed scarves and ties, bookends, jewelry, key chains, nightlights, ornaments, and much more are available in gift shops.

Not all products that use the image or form of the Capitol focus seriously on its symbolic meaning. Some people might feel, for example, that Capitol-shaped salt-and-pepper shakers are silly or disrespectful of the democratic ideals the building represents. But others would say that such items are all created in good fun, and just express how much people love and treasure the U.S. Capitol, a national **symbol** of unity, **democracy**, and freedom.

Souvenirs of the Capitol remain popular.

Timeline

1790	Congress decides that a permanent capital city will be located on the Potomac River
1791	George Washington picks specific site on Potomac for new capital
1793	William Thornton wins contest for the Capitol building with his classical design featuring two separate wings and a center dome decorated with Greek columns
1793	President George Washington lays the cornerstone and construction begins
1800	Congress, the Library of Congress, and the Supreme Court move into the unfinished building; only North wing is complete
1814	In the War of 1812, British soldiers capture Washington, D.C., and set fire to the Capitol
1855	Congress votes to enlarge building and replace original dome
1863	Statue of Freedom raised into place on top of dome
1890s	Electricity installed and plumbing updated
1950-90	Modern restoration starts to maintain building; West front is extended; paint on dome is removed and repainted in time for President John F. Kennedy's inauguration
1993	Restoration of Statue of Freedom project begins
2000	Construction of Capitol Visitors Center begins

Further Information

Congressional Pages

During each session of Congress, high school students work as pages, or assistants, for the House and Senate. Congressional pages run errands for members of Congress, set up podiums for speakers, and generally help out in the **chambers**. They also distribute the many copies of current bills that are printed in the Document Room. If you are interested in becoming a page one day, you should contact your local representative or senator.

To find your Sentator go to www.senate.gov/senators/index.cfm
To find your Representative go to www.house.gov/writerep

To find out more about the page program go to:
http://www.pagealumni.us/congpageassoc/frameindex.htm

Further Reading

Britton, Tamara. *The Capitol*. Edina, Minn: Abdo, 2003.

Feldman, Ruth. *How Congress Works: A Look at the Legislative Branch*. Minneapolis: Lerner, 2003.

Giddens-White, Bryon. *Congress and the Legislative Branch*. Chicago: Heinemann, 2006.

Glossary

amateur person who does an activity for fun, not for pay

architect person who designs buildings and other large structures

architecture art of designing and building structures

barracks housing for soldiers

chamber room or a hall for meetings

debate formal argument

democracy form of government where all people have an equal voice

galleries narrow balconies or long halls

legislative law-making

patriotic showing a love for and pride in one's country

rotunda large, round room

seceded officially withdrawn

symbol something that stands for something else

Index